# THE POWER OF FAITH

## BY
## BRANDON HUFFMAN

Philippians 4:13 "For I can do everything through Christ, who gives me strength."-NLT

# *Table of Contents*

# *PRELUDE*

In the beginning, I want to clarify that before my heart issues were diagnosed, I had lived a very healthy life with zero signs of cardiac-related problems. Plus, there was no history of heart problems in my family, so the diagnosis you are going to read came from out of nowhere.

The day I found out I had heart problems, it was not only a surprise for me but quite a shock. Imagine starting your day like any other normal day. It was a cool, crisp morning, which is usually regarded as the perfect for deer hunting. I put on extra layers and bundled up against the morning chill, starting the walk towards my favorite sitting spot. It was about a 50-yard walk up and down hills, with muddy ditches and through dense underbrush. The journey was brisk, as the cold air filled my lungs, and the crunch of leaves under my feet could be easily heard.

I felt fine when I got to the clearing, so I sat for about three hours. The atmosphere was serene; you could see a little of your breath getting scraped, and the early morning mist gripped the trees like a delicate scarf. Squirrels were rustling in the trees above me and running after one another playfully, and you could hear the turkeys gobbling and waking up from a distance. The serenity of nature was almost therapeutic, a total break from the usual bustling life of the city. The forest came alive with the roaring sounds of wildlife. These sounds made me feel that I was not entirely alone in that beautiful landscape.

At last, after seeing nothing the whole time, I decided to head back to the house. My body felt tired but satisfied from the time spent outdoors. When I got back to the house, I was completely exhausted and out of breath. I thought I was short of breath because of the amount of clothes that I had on, the thick layers making it hard for me to move freely and breathe deeply. So, I changed into comfortable sweatpants and relaxed in my chair. The warmth of the house and the softness of the chair were a welcome relief. After a while, I started feeling less lightheaded and began to feel better. The calm of the evening seemed to lull me into a false sense of security.

However, when it was 10 at night, while I was getting ready for bed, I felt a sharp pain on the right side of my chest. The pain was sudden and stabbing, severe enough to take my breath. I initially thought it was my appendix, and hence, we hurriedly headed to the ER at Sullivan County Memorial Hospital (SCMH). The drive at that point felt like an eternity, every bump in the road rippling waves of pain through my body.

The nurses at the ER started running tests to figure out what was causing the pain. While they were running the tests and waiting for the results, they hooked me up to monitors and kept an eye on my vitals. The ER's bright and sterile lights, the soft beeping of the monitors, and the jostle of the medical staff created a surreal environment. The monitors depicted a very high pulse rate and were going in and out of atrial fibrillation (AFib), which is an irregular and often very rapid heart rhythm. An irregular heart rhythm is called arrhythmia.

The nurses injected every heart medication they could think of at me to bring my heart rate somehow down. They were very quick, and their calm professionalism was indeed very commendable given the chaotic circumstances for me.

When nothing worked, the staff at the hospital concluded that I needed to be transported to a bigger hospital that would have more resources to identify and treat my condition. The only nearest hospital that had an open ER bed was Boone Hospital. The urgency in the nurses' voices and the speed at which they moved filled me with a mounting sense of trepidation. When my heart rate fell to a point where it was safe for me to be transported, I was loaded into an ambulance and taken on a one-hour trip to the Boone. The ride was a blur of flashing lights and sirens, the faces of the paramedics hovering over me as monitoring my condition pulse by pulse.

When I arrived at Boone, I was immediately taken to the ICU and hooked up to monitors so nurses and doctors could see what my heart rate was doing. The ICU was tumultuous, with medical staff moving quickly around me. The blood tests they performed revealed that because of the AFib, a blood clot had formed around my heart. The doctors immediately administered blood thinners, hoping the clot would dissolve and pass naturally into the bloodstream. The waiting was agonizing as each passing moment was full of fear that the clot would move and settle somewhere vital before the medication had a chance to work.

Unfortunately, what I feared happened. Before the clot could dissolve, it dislodged and moved to my brain, causing the first ischemic stroke attack. The world was slowing down as I felt the effects of the stroke take hold. The doctors took me to the operating room to remove the clot before too much damage had been done. The rush to the operating room was a flurry of movement with urgent voices in my ears and the medical staff working with incredible speed and precision around me.

After a while, I remember waking up to a perfect feeling, almost as if nothing had happened. The relief was overwhelming, and for a brief moment, I thought the worst was over out of the ICU and on the rehabilitation floor. I was able to recollect different conversations and discovered that I was on the verge of heart failure, but I started recovering and never got worse. If it had gotten worse or didn't improve, then the doctors were going to put me on the transplant list. Because of the serenity and professionalism of the doctors and staff around me, I never realized I was still in the ICU.

However, the problem was far from over. I don't recall for how long I remained conscious until the second stroke, which was hemorrhagic, occurred. I remember having a conversation with my cardiologist when she suddenly noticed the signs of another stroke. Her face turned pale as she urgently called for assistance. Seconds later, I was rushed to the OR once again. Despite the doctors' rapid actions, by the time I reached the operation room, damage to the right side of my brain had already occurred. The world around me appeared to become totally blurred, with the colors of life fading.

The aftermath of the second stroke was difficult and complex. The damage to the right side of my brain had affected my motor skills and speech. It was like I was trapped in my own body. The following days were filled with never-ending tests, scans, and consultations with various specialists. The doctors and nurses were extremely supportive, but my condition was a heavy and delicate burden to bear.

Rehabilitation was a slow and arduous process. I had to relearn how to perform basic tasks I had once taken for granted. Physical therapy sessions were painful, as for every move, I had to push my limits to regain strength and coordination. Each small victory, whether it was taking a step without assistance or articulating a coherent sentence, was a tough battle.

The emotional toll was immense, and I could remember those days when things got overwhelming to the extent that I was engulfed with a sense of dread that I would never be able to go back to my original position. My friends and family remained close to me; hence, they became my sole support system. Their love and faith regarding my recovery was one thing that made me survive that darkest period of my life.

As I progressed through my recovery, I began understanding the importance of patience and perseverance. Each setback was a reminder of the fragility of life and the strength required to overcome adversity. I learned to celebrate the small milestones and to focus on the progress I was making, no matter how slow it seemed.

Throughout my journey of recovery, I understood the significance of patience and perseverance. I became familiar with how to overcome adversity, no matter how difficult or slow the process is.

The experience gave me a sense of life, making me feel the importance of friends and family. The people around me who loved me despite I was of low productivity to them. I was vulnerable, yet they consoled me and stayed beside me every moment.

To reduce the risk of future strokes and my heart condition, I had to make strict lifestyle changes. This included a strict medication regimen, regular check-ups with my cardiologist, and adopting a healthier diet and exercise regimen. These changes felt challenging at first, but eventually, I adapted to my new way of life.

Despite all the difficulties and challenges, when I look back at those days, I am grateful for the lessons I learned and the challenges I embraced. The diagnosis that was once a sudden and devastating blow became a motivation factor for personal growth and having a deeper appreciation for life.

Now, as I continue with my life, I feel very powerful and committed. My worldview is now more holistic, and I can see things with deeper understanding and nuances.

# Chapter One

# The Awakening

I was lying in the sterile, white room of the Boone Hospital, caught in dusk between consciousness and a drug-induced murk. The machine was beeping rhythmically, the beeps being continuous in their melody. It was 19th November 2021, while I was in the fog of recovery from a stroke that had cruelly attacked mainly the right side of my brain. Before this, my life was as a $5^{th}$-standard math teacher. It was a one-hour drive to the South Harrison High School. I used to really enjoy it as it was a therapeutic drive that prepared me to train young minds to develop their analytical skills. After a long day at school, I would listen to my favorite music and unwind from my day.

When I was lying half asleep, the first sign that something was erroneous came from my sensation and not from a doctor's explanation. My left arm draped over my stomach and felt numb, as though it belonged to someone else. Panic fluttered in my chest as I tried to reconcile the feeling with any understanding or a guess. This was my introduction to left-side neglect, a cruel trick played by my brain due to the damage on its right side. At that moment, I realized the physical reality of my condition as it crashed into me swiftly. A cruel trick caused by the stroke; the physical therapists said I needed to be careful around hot items because I had no feeling on my left side. To demonstrate this, they had me close my eyes and raise my hand when I felt them touch my left leg. When the test was over, they said I only felt them touch my leg 40% of the time.

I grew up on a small farm in northern Missouri and, therefore, was familiar with living under stringent conditions that shaped me into a resilient being. Being the oldest of three siblings, I always had this huge bar of responsibility over my shoulders. My upbringing was such that my day consisted of hard labor, occasional escapades to the basketball court, and running along tracks. But all of this could not prepare me for the condition I was in on the hospital bed.

I spent seventeen days in the ICU with continuous therapy sessions for my speech, motor skills, and occupation-related issues, and it was as if I went back to school and all my therapists were my instructors guiding me through the grueling process of relearning the basic tasks. During these sessions, whenever I struggled to walk without a cane or tried to dress independently, I truly understood the power of perseverance.

My faith became a cornerstone of my existence, providing me with a wellspring of strength. "God gives me the strength to persevere and never give up through the hard times of PT and OT." This became my mantra. The encouragement from my family, the unwavering support of my friends, and the dedication of the medical staff acted as pillars to hold me up, as if they were the reason I was gaining a sense of life.

The ICU was a place of rush and chaos, the nurses and doctors going here and there, their footsteps were echoing and forming a unique melody alongside the beeps of life support machines. The smell of anti-septic sanitizers was abundant, and my life was hanging between dismay and a slight hope for recovery. My bed was surrounded by machines, and my every pulse and every breath were monitored. It was the environment that made me contemplate the fragility of human life.

My family used to visit often, and their presence was very comforting. However, I could see the mixture of confusion and determination on their faces. My siblings, who had always looked up to me, supported me, making me immensely proud. Each visit by them was filled with family and home stories, updates on what was going on outside, and, of course, a short speech on how soon I would join in living life outside the hospital.

As the days turned into weeks, I started to recover at a better pace. I regained some sense, and things started to become normal. The therapy sessions were, however, quite exhausting, and they pushed me to my physical and emotional limits. It is also important to mention that my therapists were incredible. Their patience was remarkable and they were quite aware of what I used to feel for every step I managed to relearn. They pushed me when I needed to be pushed and encouraged me when I felt defeated. They celebrated every little milestone I took.

The emotional toll of the stroke was as challenging as the physical recovery. But these were the precise moments when I found strength in my faith and the support of my loved ones. My prayers became a source of solace, and my belief in God grew stronger. I could see that my suffering was just not meaningless, and there was some sense and greater meaning to it, which was intended as such by God.

Finally, on 13th January 2022, I departed from the hospital. I entered a world that felt both familiar and alien. I could feel the simple joys of living at home, the joys maybe I used to take for granted. The smell of fresh coffee in the morning, the warm bed, the liberty to sit at my chair beside the window, and whatnot. Though I wasn't granted full clearance to return to teaching, the prospect of standing in front of a classroom again and sharing knowledge with the young minds somehow became fuel to my recovery.

## The Awakening

As I was having plenty of time to contemplate, I looked toward the future. Hence, I applied for the Master's program at Northwest Missouri State University. I got accepted into the **Curriculum & Instruction: Teaching Technology** program, which was indeed a solid step towards growing my career in the field of training and education.

Applying for a master's program wasn't easy. It was challenging and daunting. However, most importantly, it was a step towards finding myself and creating a purpose for my new life. This path could lead me back into academics and equip me with skills that would benefit many people around me.

As I am writing these words, I am looking forward to completing my Master's degree in December of 2024.

## The Awakening

The journey that started from a hospital bed to here doing my master's is a tumult in itself, but I am enjoying it since it has a purpose and hope. The scars of my stroke are not just marks of survival; they are proof of my transformation, which was fueled by faith and an untiring determination to return to my calling. In the darkest times, I somehow managed to find the brightest of lights.

These experiences gave me a new perspective on teaching. Now, I understand the challenges my students face in great depth. I can feel their anxiety and confusion; I can see that desperation to know how a problem can be solved in the easiest yet most logical way possible. The classes I take now are full of intuitions, and my teaching style has become extremely conducive and empathic. I can see potential in every student sitting right in front of me, which gives me more power and hope.

The master's program gave me a lot of new thought and has been an incredible journey of learning and growth. The professors have been supportive and I learn a lot from my classmates and their unique experiences. The classroom experience, but as a student has been tremendous as it allows me to be the one asking questions and reflecting on differing views.

As I am looking forward to completing my degree, I am equipped with an incredible sense of accomplishment. I am super excited about the future and always think of opportunities ahead. I see myself as a hope to change the lives of my students.

## The Awakening

The journey from the hospital to here has been long, but it taught me a lot. It gave me a sense of joy, growth, and transformation. At last, my journey is more than just a recovery. It was a learning curve where I discovered the true meaning of love, support, friendship, and fear. As I move forward, I intend to carry with me the lessons learned. I believe that the strength I gained during this process has been vital in making me strive for my dreams.

Glory and praise to God. It is through His strength and the support of my loved ones that I have come this far. With God's guidance and the love of my family, I sincerely believe that even If I take little steps, one at a time, my future is bejeweled with hope, strength, and purpose. I wish to inspire many out there who think their life

## The Awakening

has no meaning or perhaps it is irrecoverable but

in true essence, life is a journey, a journey to find

your own true potential.

# Chapter 2
## Senior Year

Since Newtown-Harris R-III High School was a small school district, the number of sports students could participate in was limited. During my senior year, I chose to play basketball and run track. These decisions were driven by a passion for athletics and a desire to make the most of my final year in high school.

The basketball team that year had several talented freshmen on the roster, injecting new energy and potential into the team. Our coach, Coach Cool, had a knack for spotting raw talent and molding it into something formidable. Practices were grueling but rewarding. We spent hours running drills, perfecting our shots, and strategizing our plays. The camaraderie we built was second to none, and it was clear that this was a special group.

The season started strong, with the team quickly establishing itself as a contender in the conference. Our success was not just due to our physical abilities but also our mental toughness and determination. One of my favorite memories from the basketball season was winning the conference tournament. The gym was packed for the championship game, and the atmosphere was electric. The game was close the entire time, with neither team able to pull away. It all came down to the final seconds. Our post player made a buzzer-beater shot that clinched the victory for us. The entire gym erupted with excitement. It was a moment that encapsulated the spirit and effort of our team.

Another unforgettable moment happened during an away game against our biggest rivals. The tension was palpable as both teams fought fiercely for the upper hand. I remember the deafening cheers from the opposing fans and the pressure weighing heavily on our shoulders. Despite the intense environment, we managed to stay focused and played with precision and heart. In the final quarter, I executed a critical steal and passed the ball to our shooting guard, who nailed a three-pointer. This pivotal play turned the tide in our favor, and we secured a hard-fought victory. The bus ride home was filled with jubilation and a sense of pride that we had overcome such a formidable challenge. This team won districts, but our bid for state champions was unfortunately cut short after a hard-fought loss at sectionals.

Our coach always emphasized the importance of discipline and teamwork. He always wanted us to look nice when we walked into an opponent's gym, so he required us to wear dress pants or khakis; a tie was preferred. One home game, a tradition started where we would go to a teammate's house before every home game, hang out until game time, and ride to the game together. These get-togethers not only strengthened our bond but also allowed us to relax and strategize for the upcoming game. We would share laughs, discuss our dreams, and plan our plays. This ritual became a cornerstone of our team's unity and success.

## Senior Year

While basketball provided a team dynamic, track and field offered a different kind of challenge. I was a distance runner, competing in the 1600 and 3200 meters. Distance running is as much about mental fortitude as it is about physical endurance. The discipline required to maintain a steady pace, to push through the pain, and to stay focused on the finish line taught me valuable life lessons.

Coach Parsons was instrumental in my development as a runner. He had an uncanny ability to push me to my limits while ensuring I remained injury-free. Under his guidance, I improved my time significantly. One of the pivotal moments of the track season was the conference meet. To help score points and secure a win for our team, Coach had me run in the 800, 1600,

3200, and the 4X800 relay. The conference meeting was held on a freezing day, and I remember wanting to get through my events as quickly as possible so I could put my sweats back on and get warm.

A particularly memorable event occurred during the districts. The weather was uncooperative, with heavy rain turning the track into a slippery mess. Many competitors struggled with the conditions, but Coach Parsons always told us to be prepared for anything. He had us practice in various weather conditions, and that preparation paid off. I managed to maintain my footing and kept a steady pace throughout the race. In the final lap of the 1600 meters, I surged ahead and finished the race. The sense of accomplishment I felt crossing the finish line was unparalleled.

During one of our regular track practices, an unexpected event occurred that tested our resilience. We were in the middle of interval training when a severe storm rolled in. The sky darkened, and the wind picked up, making it impossible to continue. Coach Parsons decided to move the practice indoors. We ended up doing stair drills and core exercises in the gym. Despite the disruption, we adapted and made the most of the situation. This experience taught us the importance of flexibility and perseverance in the face of adversity.

The climax of the track season was the state championship meet. Qualifying for this event was a goal I had set at the beginning of the year, and achieving it felt like the culmination of all my hard work. The competition was fierce, with the best runners from across the state vying for the top spots. I competed in the 4x800 relay, determined to give my best performance. In the 4x800 relay, I managed to set a personal record by cutting 30 seconds off of my time from the district meet to the state meet. Although the team didn't win, I felt an immense sense of accomplishment. It was a fitting end to my high school athletic career.

One of the unexpected highlights of the state meet was meeting athletes from other schools who shared my passion for running. We exchanged stories, training tips, and encouragement. These interactions broadened my perspective and made me realize that the world of sports is a vast and supportive community. Even though we were competitors, there was a mutual respect and admiration that transcended the race.

Reflecting on my senior year, I realize that the experiences on the basketball court and the track were more than just about sports. They were about growth, resilience, and the bonds formed with teammates and coaches. The lessons I learned about teamwork, leadership, and perseverance have stayed with me long after graduation.

Basketball taught me the importance of trust and collaboration. Each player had a role; success depended on how well we worked together. The thrill of winning both the conference and district championships and the joy of celebrating with my teammates are memories that will always hold a special place in my heart.

Track and field, on the other hand, taught me about individual determination and the power of the mind. The long hours of training, the solitary nature of distance running, and the satisfaction of personal improvement were all part of a journey that built my character and strengthened my resolve.

My senior year at Newtown-Harris R-III High School was filled with challenges and triumphs. It was a year that defined my athletic career and set the stage for my future endeavors. The experiences I gained and the lessons I learned continue to influence me, reminding me of the value of hard work, dedication, and the support of a close-knit community.

## Senior Year

Senior year was a time of tremendous growth, both personally and athletically. The memories forged during this period are etched in my mind, serving as constant reminders of my prowess and growth.

# Chapter 3

## Transitional Summer

It was the summer before I would attend North Central Missouri College (NCMC). Determined to save up for my first semester, I decided to get a job and managed to secure one mowing the grounds of a local farming organization. The days were long and hot, but that didn't deter me from my goal. Despite the grueling hours under the scorching sun, I had grown up learning not to leave a job unfinished. There were days when I felt like quitting early, but I chose to stick it out and finish what I had started. This job taught me a valuable lesson about perseverance and resilience.

## Transitional Summer

Mowing became a form of therapy for me. The constant hum of the mower and the smell of freshly cut grass provided a soothing rhythm that helped me clear my mind. During these long mowing hours, I began to contemplate my future. The idea of starting my own mowing business after college began to take shape in my mind. The satisfaction of seeing a well-mowed lawn gave me a sense of accomplishment and pride in my work.

After working tirelessly for several weeks, I finally accumulated enough vacation days to take some time off. One day, while taking a break with my coworkers Billy and Walter, I overheard them discussing an upcoming trip to Florida. Jokingly, I asked if I could join them, and to my surprise, they agreed. Walter's vehicle was in the shop, so he proposed that he would cover all the expenses if we took my car. This was an offer I couldn't refuse.

Our journey to Florida was filled with excitement and anticipation. For me, it was my first time venturing so far from home and seeing the Atlantic Ocean. As we drove closer to the coast, the landscape began to change. Palm trees lined the streets, and the air carried a salty tang. When we finally arrived, and I stepped onto the beach, I was mesmerized by the vast expanse of the ocean. The feel of the warm beach sand between my toes was a sensation I had never experienced before. Despite my efforts to brush the sand off before getting back into the car, it clung to everything, a persistent reminder of the beach.

## Transitional Summer

We found a hotel with a decent price that offered a spectacular view of the ocean. Each of us had our own room, and I remember sitting on my balcony, listening to the sound of the waves crashing on the shore. The cool breeze from the ocean was refreshing, and I watched in awe as massive container ships sailed into the nearby port. The highlight of my trip was witnessing my first ocean sunset. The sun, a brilliant orb of orange, slowly dipped below the horizon, casting a mesmerizing array of colors across the sky and water. The city buzzed with activity, but the sight of the sunset brought a sense of peace and calmness over me.

The days in Florida flew by, filled with exploration and relaxation. We visited local attractions, tried new foods, and soaked up the sun on the beach. One day, we took a boat tour that offered a closer look at the marine life and the sprawling coastal scenery. The boat's gentle sway and the ocean's expanse were incredibly tranquil, offering a new perspective on the world. We also ventured into the bustling city life, visiting shops and experiencing the area's vibrant culture.

Unfortunately, all good things must come to an end, and our Florida vacation was no exception. The trip back to Missouri was bittersweet. I felt a mix of contentment from my experiences and a longing to return. Back in Missouri, I resumed my job, carrying with me memories of the ocean and the lessons I had learned during my time away. The sand, still lingering in my car, reminded me of our adventures.

## Transitional Summer

As summer came to a close, it was time to prepare for my new chapter at NCMC. I had to quit my mowing job, but the experiences and lessons I gained stayed with me. The dream of starting my own mowing business remained, but now I was focused on my studies and the opportunities that lay ahead at college.

Despite the vacation being cut short, it left a lasting impression on me. The trip to Florida was not just a getaway but a journey of self-discovery and growth. I had ventured out of my comfort zone, experienced new things, and learned the importance of balancing work and relaxation. I promised myself that I would return to Florida one day to explore more and relive the serenity of the beach and the ocean.

## Transitional Summer

The summer before college had been a transitional period, preparing me mentally and emotionally for future changes. My experiences at work and during my vacation shaped my outlook and provided a strong foundation for the future. As I stepped into my first semester at NCMC, I carried with me the resilience, determination, and a sense of adventure that would guide me through my college years and beyond.

# Chapter 4

## Blind-Sided

Isn't it true that life sometimes seems to have its own twists and turns, more than a little unpredictably? Just when we think we've got things sorted out, BAM! That sense of being in control goes away like magic. The very randomness or unpredictability of it all makes one marvel.

Upon recovering from my stroke, I found myself at a crossroads. The idea of teaching 5th-grade math again was both reassuring and terrifying. Reassuring because this was a world I knew well, where I had once found joy in helping mold young minds. Frightening because it figured prominently among all those questions I couldn't seem to stop asking myself, as well as fears for the future that infused my entire being during those many months spent at hospitals on my back. But life has its way of urging us to embrace the unfamiliar with open arms. And so, with a mixture of fear and joy, I applied for a job at the local high school, hoping that I would get a chance to be a teacher again.

It still feels like yesterday when I first walked into that classroom on my first day, and all my apprehension was gone. The students before me seemed uncertain: Was it skepticism or curiosity? We were all beginning this journey together and could not say what lay ahead.

Teaching 5th-grade math was both a pleasure and a headache. The subject matter itself was familiar ground, but the classroom dynamics were another story altogether. Each student had his or her own unique approach to life and its share of strengths and weaknesses. Now, it was my job to impart information and create a place where they felt supported and inspired.

The catch was that the school was located an hour away. I had to hop in my car and drive for a whole hour just to get there. But you know what? Despite the long drive, I genuinely enjoyed every minute of being at that school. The sight of face after face full of eagerness in those classrooms was like a breath of fresh air: it's impossible to feel down when you are with children who are enthusiastic and ready to learn. I felt that through me, they would break the bounds of ignorance, light up their living habits, and say: "Yes, that's real math!" The students' "aha!" moments were more magical than anything else.

My first weeks at South Harrison were a whirlwind of activity. I had to relearn the rhythm of a school day, get to know my colleagues and understand the school's unique culture. The administration was supportive, and my fellow teachers were welcoming. They shared tips and advice, which made my transition smoother. I quickly realized that the heart of teaching wasn't just about the lessons and the relationships we build with our students and colleagues.

One particular student, Jenny, stands out in my memory. She struggled with math and had little confidence in her abilities. I worked with her daily, breaking down problems into manageable steps and encouraging her to believe in herself. Slowly but surely, Jenny's confidence grew. One day, she solved a problem on the board that had stumped the entire class. The look of triumph on her face was priceless. Moments like these made the long drive and the challenges of teaching worthwhile.

Another student, Tom, was the class clown. Always quick with a joke, he often disrupted lessons. However, beneath his playful exterior, Tom had a sharp mind. By channeling his energy into productive outlets, like helping him lead group activities and encouraging him to assist his peers, I was able to harness his potential. Tom flourished and became a positive influence in the classroom.

As the months went by, I noticed changes in myself, too. My confidence returned, and my passion for teaching was reignited. I looked forward to each day, excited to see what new challenges and triumphs awaited. The drive to South Harrison became a time of reflection and preparation, a quiet hour where I could plan lessons and think about my students' progress.

In the spring, the school held a math fair. Each class was tasked with creating projects that showcased their understanding of various mathematical concepts. My students were enthusiastic about the event, and we spent weeks preparing. They worked on everything from geometry and fractions to probability and statistics. On the day of the fair, the gymnasium was filled with colorful displays, and the air was buzzing with excitement. Parents and teachers walked from booth to booth, admiring the students' work.

Blind-Sided

Seeing my students confidently explain their projects to visitors was immensely gratifying. It was a testament to their hard work and my efforts to make math engaging and accessible. The pride on their faces as they received compliments and praise was heartwarming. It was a highlight of the school year and a reminder of why I had chosen to teach.

Outside the classroom, I tried to get involved in the school community. I attended sports events, school plays, and parent-teacher meetings. These activities allowed me to build stronger connections with my students and their families. I learned about their lives outside school, hopes and dreams, and challenges. This deeper understanding helped me tailor my teaching to meet better and support their needs.

Blind-Sided

One memorable event was the school's annual field day. It was a day filled with games, races, and friendly competition. I volunteered to help organize the activities and even participated in a few races. The students were thrilled to see their teachers joining in the fun. Laughter and cheers filled the air as we competed in sack, tug-of-war, and relay races. It was a day of joy and camaraderie, strengthening the bond between teachers and students.

As the school year drew close, I reflected on my journey. The transition from recovery to teaching had been challenging, but it had also been incredibly rewarding. I had rediscovered my love for teaching and had formed meaningful connections with my students. The experience taught me the importance of resilience, patience, and compassion. It has shown me that we can find strength and purpose even in the face of adversity.

Leaving South Harrison at the end of the school year was bittersweet. I had grown attached to my students and colleagues, and saying goodbye was difficult. However, I knew I was leaving a piece of myself with them and taking a part of them with me. The lessons we had learned together, the challenges we had overcome, and the moments of joy and triumph would stay with me forever.

In the end, life had indeed thrown me a curveball, but it had also allowed me to grow, reconnect with my passion, and make a difference in the lives of others. As I looked forward to the next chapter, I carried with me the memories and experiences of my time at South Harrison, knowing that they had shaped me into a better teacher and a stronger person.

What happened was that my first year of teaching was cut short without warning. I wound up with a diagnosis of atrial fibrillation—a fancy term for battering, fluttering heartbeats. Next thing I knew, I found myself in the ICU at Boone Hospital, rigged up to an assortment of machines and monitors.

An innovation of the plot! From standing in front of a whiteboard to lying in a hospital bed, I was thinking of my students at South Harrison High School, filled with uncertainty and wanting to go back to them. It wasn't easy, to put it mildly. Charmingly, when life gives you lemons, don't actually turn them all into lemonade; try planting the seeds at least.

After a tiring day, when I was at home, I began to experience some strange symptoms. My heart fluttered. Its actual rhythm was scattered. The uneasy feeling was overpowering. Before I knew what had happened, I found myself in Boone Hospital's Intensive Care Unit (ICU), my home away from home. It was utterly sterile and clinically bland. At that time, in the ICU, my thoughts often returned to my students. How were they? Did they miss me standing before the Smartboard while challenging them with algebraic terms and equations? Despite myself, I longed to be with them, to continue pushing their education further.

## Blind-Sided

But life has its own plans for us at times, and we have to take them as they come. In that room, filled with beeping machines and walls painted a sterile white color, I could not help but reflect on just how unpredictable life really is. It does not always follow the script we have carefully written. It contains twists and turns, leaving us feeling disoriented and vulnerable. Yet, in those moments of uncertainty, our true character and resilience can shine through.

On November 19, 2021, I was diagnosed with atrial fibrillation—a heart condition that causes the rhythm of heartbeats to become irregular. It was a revelation that brought new challenges. The cause was unknown at that time.

There I lay, within the walls of Boone Hospital, which pulsed with strange sounds originating from places unknown. This was a paradox. Great technological possibilities were lightly shrouded in mist, their ugliness entirely overshadowed by what they meant. Helplessness hung in the air. As they plugged this line into me and that wire into the other diagnostic equipment, including a heart rate monitor that was connected by wires and nodes hanging about me, I felt dreadfully vulnerable.

From my once vivid teaching career to a promising future now lost in the deep night of uncertainty, my work was in suspended animation. It felt as if someone had pushed the pause button on my life; I groped my way like a blind man in darkness. But deep within this hopelessness, a tiny spark of vitality ignited. I was determined to recover and find my way back to the classroom and my students. That tiny spark of vitality grew into a flame of determination. I knew I had to get back to what I loved, the students who needed me, and the life that awaited me outside those hospital walls.

As I lay in the hospital bed, memories of my teaching days flooded my mind. I remembered the excitement of the first day of school, the joy of seeing students' faces light up when they understood a difficult concept, and the satisfaction of helping them grow. Those memories fueled my desire to get better. I began to set small goals for myself, starting with sitting up in bed, then walking a few steps, and eventually walking around the ward. Each small achievement was a step closer to my goal of returning to the classroom.

## Blind-Sided

The hospital staff were incredibly supportive. The nurses and doctors encouraged me every step of the way. They became my cheerleaders, celebrating each milestone with me. Their kindness and compassion reminded me of the importance of human connection, a lesson I had always tried to impart to my students. I realized that just as my students needed me, I needed them. Their energy, curiosity, and enthusiasm for learning have always been a source of strength for me.

One day, while walking around the ward, I met a fellow patient named George. He was an older gentleman who had suffered a heart attack. Despite his own struggles, he had a positive outlook on life. We quickly became friends, sharing stories about our lives and our hopes for the future. George's resilience and optimism were contagious. He reminded me that we can choose our attitude even in the face of adversity. His friendship was a blessing during my hospital stay.

As the weeks passed, I continued to make progress. I attended physical therapy sessions to regain my strength and participated in support groups where I met others who were going through similar experiences. These sessions were both physically and emotionally challenging, but they were also incredibly rewarding. I learned to appreciate the small victories and to be patient with myself. Healing, I realized, was not a linear process. There were good days and bad days, but each day brought me closer to my goal.

Finally, the day came when I was discharged from the hospital. It was a moment of triumph but also a moment of reflection. I had been given a second chance and determined to make the most of it. Returning home was both comforting and overwhelming. The familiar surroundings were a stark contrast to the sterile hospital environment. I was grateful to be back, but I knew that the road to recovery was far from over.

I continued my rehabilitation at home, focusing on building my physical and mental strength. I practiced mindfulness and meditation to calm my mind and reduce stress. I also reconnected with friends and family, who had supported me throughout my ordeal. Their love and encouragement were invaluable, reminding me I was not alone in my journey.

As I regained my strength, I began preparing to return to teaching. I reached out to my colleagues at South Harrison High School, who would've welcomed me back with open arms, but unfortunately, there were no teacher openings when I had recovered enough to get back to teaching. They had kept me in their thoughts and prayers, and their support meant the world to me. I remember feeling joy after receiving a slew of get-well cards from my students.

I was actively seeking a teaching position in one of the local school districts, with a particular interest in teaching accounting and computer applications. These subjects are academically enriching and highly practical, allowing students to apply what they learn directly to real-life situations. My enthusiasm for these topics stemmed from their relevance and the tangible impact they could have on students' future careers and everyday lives. I found it incredibly rewarding to see students understand complex concepts and know that these skills would benefit them long after they left the classroom. However, if I had been unable to secure a teaching position, I would have been equally passionate about the idea of starting my own tutoring business. This would have allowed me to provide personalized support to students in these critical areas, ensuring that they had the opportunity to excel regardless of the classroom setting.

My passion for teaching developed during my two to three years as a substitute teacher. This experience was gratifying, as I had the opportunity to help students who were struggling to grasp certain concepts. Working one-on-one with these students and seeing the moment when they finally understood and could solve the problems on their own was profoundly satisfying. These experiences solidified my desire to pursue teaching as a career and underscored the importance of patience, creativity, and dedication in education. I recall the joy and pride I felt when students who had been struggling began to improve and gain confidence in their abilities. This hands-on experience taught me invaluable lessons about the diverse needs of students and how to adapt my teaching methods to meet those needs effectively.

I initially started to substitute teaching to earn some money while I was still in school because it gave me flexibility in my schedule. This flexibility allowed me to balance my academic responsibilities while gaining valuable teaching experience. After completing college, I continued to substitute teach as I searched for a full-time teaching position. This ongoing experience not only honed my teaching skills but also deepened my commitment to education and my desire to impact students' academic journeys. Substitute teaching offered me a unique perspective on different classroom environments and teaching styles, which enriched my own approach to teaching. During this period, I truly realized the profound impact a dedicated teacher can have on their students, and I became more determined than ever to secure a permanent role in education.

Atrial fibrillation symptoms have little to recommend them. The arrhythmic heartbeat stirs you up like some wicked drummer. Each beat is a gamble: What will happen next? This grating lack of breath renders people breathless and helpless at once—as though all the weight in heaven was pushing down on their chest until it collapses entirely.

In those moments, something within me longed for, with a sense bordering on homesickness, to return to the classroom. I yearned to stand before my students and guide them through this world full of numbers, equations, and symbols. Nevertheless, fate may have chosen one path and several paths for me, all of which I must tread with patience. Determination and persistence to the end are required to arrive alive at a goal.

During those long, solitary nights in the hospital, it was as if the world around me faded away, leaving just me and these four walls. They had seen it all—every moment of uncertainty, every flicker of determination, every surge of fear.

Despite feeling bone-tired most of the time, when my heart decided to go rogue, I didn't face any major hurdles. It's almost surreal to admit, but I never even found myself rushing to the ER because I just didn't feel like something wasn't right with me. It was as if I was living in this strange bubble of normalcy within the chaos of fibrillation.

The news hit my parents like a bolt out of the blue. A family with no track record of heart issues suddenly confronted with the reality of cardiomyopathy. I can still picture how their faces contorted, a mix of shock and concern, as the doctor delivered the diagnosis. It was heartbreaking to see them like this. At the age when I was supposed to give them a peaceful, laid-back life, here they stood all stressed out just because of me.

In those moments, it felt like time slowed down. I could see the worry imprinted on their expressions, the lines of their faces deepening with each passing second. Questions hung heavy in the air, unspoken fears swirling around us like a storm about to break.

But during this uncertainty, there was also a fierce determination. My parents are the kind of people who don't back down from a challenge; this is what they had taught me to do. This mindset was something that prevented me from losing hope during this phase. As they wrapped their heads around this unexpected twist in our family's story, I could see the gears turning and the resolve set in.

It's funny how life throws these curveballs at you when you least expect them. You're sailing along one moment, blissfully unaware of the storm brewing on the horizon. And then, out of nowhere, comes a diagnosis that changes everything. But through it all, there's a strange comfort in knowing that we're facing this together as a family, united in our determination to weather whatever comes our way.

The desire to return to teaching became my guiding light, illuminating even the darkest moments of my rehabilitation journey. It was more than just a job—it was my passion, purpose, and essence of who I am. With each grueling session, I held onto the vision of standing again in front of my students, imparting knowledge and inspiration.

But there was something deeper driving me forward, something beyond mere determination. Call it intuition, call it divine intervention—whatever it was, I felt it stirring within me like a gentle but unwavering force. I came to know it as my "inner voice," my connection to something greater than myself. It whispered words of encouragement when my strength waned, urging me to keep pushing and believing, even when the odds seemed insurmountable.

In those moments of doubt and fatigue, this inner flame kept me going, igniting a resilience I never knew I possessed. It was as if the Holy Spirit itself had taken residence within me, guiding my steps, bolstering my resolve, and refusing to let me falter. And so, fueled by the twin fires of passion and faith, I pressed on, knowing that with each step forward, I was moving closer to the moment when I would once again answer the call of the classroom.

The decision to resign from my beloved teaching position weighed heavily on my heart. It felt like I was relinquishing a part of my identity, stepping away from something that had defined me for so long. But the reality was stark: the demands of my intensive rehabilitation schedule left little room for the classroom demands. So, with a heavy heart and a resolve born of necessity, I made the difficult choice to step back, knowing that my health had to come first. I felt like something was trapped in my throat, making me miserable.

## Blind-Sided

Relearning the essential tasks of daily life was a humbling experience. I had to learn everything from scratch, like how to walk or write. It felt a bit odd. Tasks that once came effortlessly now required painstaking effort and concentration. Simple actions like tying my shoelaces or pouring a cup of coffee became monumental challenges; each small victory was celebrated with a mixture of relief and determination.

One of the most brutal blows came when I attempted to write for the first time since the stroke. My once-flawless handwriting, a source of pride and precision, now appeared as a chaotic jumble of shaky lines and illegible scrawls. It was a bitter reminder of all that I had lost, a tangible symbol of the stroke's devastating impact on my life.

However, amid the frustration and despair, a spark of hope flickered. I refused to accept defeat, clinging to the belief that I could reclaim what had been taken from me with time and effort. And so, armed with determination and a steely resolve, I embarked on a rehabilitation journey, one pen stroke at a time.

It was a slow and arduous process, fraught with frustration and setbacks. There were moments when I felt like giving up when the weight of my own limitations threatened to overwhelm me. But through sheer perseverance and an unwavering belief in my own potential, I persevered.

Today, my handwriting may not be quite as flawless as it once was, but it bears the unmistakable imprint of determination and resilience. Each letter is a testament to the strength of the human spirit, a reminder that with perseverance and faith, even the most daunting obstacles can be overcome.

The path to recovery was filled with challenges, but each step forward brought me closer to my goal. I knew that returning to the classroom would not be easy, but I was determined to make it happen. With the support of my family, friends, and healthcare team, I gradually regained my strength and confidence.

We often face unexpected challenges that test our strength and resilience in life. My experience with atrial fibrillation was one such challenge. It took me from the classroom to the hospital bed and hopefully back again. Throughout this journey, I learned valuable lessons about the importance of human connection, the power of a

Blind-Sided

positive attitude, and the strength that comes from

within. I aim to teach with renewed purpose, ready

to inspire and guide my students once more.

# Chapter 5

## Turning the Tide

"Jesus looked at them and said, 'With man, this is impossible, but not with God; all things are possible with God.'" - Mark 10:27

The sterile white walls of the ICU seemed to close in on me, a constant reminder of my confinement. The rhythmic beeping of the machines became a soundtrack to my days, a pendulum marking the passage of time in this strange, new world. Yet, amidst the monotony, a spark of defiance flickered within me. I would not let this setback define me.

Days turned into weeks, and the initial shock of my diagnosis began to fade. The doctors explained that my atrial fibrillation was caused by cardiomyopathy, a condition affecting the heart muscle. The treatment plan involved medication, lifestyle changes, and a procedure called cardiac ablation to correct the irregular electrical signals in my heart.

The prospect of surgery was daunting, but I knew it was necessary. As I lay in the hospital bed, I found solace in the unwavering support of my family and friends. Their visits brought laughter and warmth to my sterile surroundings, reminding me of the love that awaited me beyond these walls.

The day of the ablation arrived, and I felt a mix of trepidation and anticipation. The first procedure was not a success, which kind of disappointed me. I went in for the procedure again, which was finally a success. After a few days of the second procedure, I was back in my home, albeit with a new appreciation for life's simple pleasures.

The road to recovery was long and demanding. The medication had side effects that I had to adjust to, and the fatigue lingered for weeks. But with each passing day, I grew physically and mentally stronger.

I used this recovery time to reflect on my life and priorities. The experience had shaken me to my core, forcing me to confront my own mortality and the fragility of existence. It also revealed the resilience of the human spirit, the ability to find strength in adversity, and to emerge from the darkness with a renewed sense of purpose.

As I regained my health, I knew that I could not return to the classroom just yet. The demands of teaching were too great, and I needed time to heal my body and mind. Instead, I decided to use my experience to help others.

I reached out to organizations supporting patients with heart conditions, offering my story and time. I wanted to speak at conferences and events, sharing my knowledge and advocating for better care and treatment, but I never got a chance.

Through these experiences, I discovered a new passion: to help others navigate the challenges of living with a chronic illness. Though difficult, I realized that my journey had equipped me with the empathy and understanding to make a difference in the lives of others.

Turning the Tide

I felt a growing sense of purpose and fulfillment as the months passed. I was no longer the same teacher who had walked into South Harrison High School on that first day. I was stronger, wiser, and more compassionate.

When the time was right, I knew I would return to the classroom, not just as a math teacher but as a guide and mentor, sharing my knowledge and the lessons I had learned on my journey through illness and recovery.

Many people find it difficult to recall exactly what their days of getting sick were; as for me, I clearly remember the date. It was November 19, 2021. I remember the day vividly, though the details remain hazy at times. A sudden, searing pain pierced my head, accompanied by a wave of dizziness that sent me crashing to the floor. My world spun, my vision blurring, and then everything went black.

When I awoke, I was surrounded by concerned faces, the worried voices of my family echoing in my ears. I learned that I had suffered an ischemic stroke caused by a blood clot blocking an artery in my brain and a hemorrhagic stroke, where a blood vessel had burst. The combination was devastating, leaving me with significant impairments.

The following days and weeks were a blur of tests, scans, and consultations. My speech was slurred, my right arm and leg paralyzed, and my memory fragmented. The doctors explained that the road to recovery would be long and demanding, but with intensive therapy and rehabilitation, I could regain some of my lost functions.

Determined to reclaim my life, I threw myself into therapy with a fierce resolve. Hours were spent relearning how to walk, talk, and perform daily tasks. Each small victory fueled my motivation, from taking a few unassisted steps to uttering a coherent sentence.

One day, I stumbled upon a stack of old photographs during an occupational therapy session. As I flipped through them, memories flooded back: my nephews and countless adventures with friends and family. It was a poignant reminder of all I had to fight for, all I had to regain.

## Turning the Tide

With each passing day, I felt myself inching closer to my old self. My speech became more explicit, my gait steadier, and my memories sharper. The road to recovery was far from smooth, punctuated by setbacks and moments of despair, but I never lost sight of my goal.

Finally, after 17 grueling days in the ICU, I was transferred to the Boone Hospital Inpatient Rehabilitation Unit. Here, I continued my intensive therapy, surrounded by a team of dedicated professionals who believed in my potential.

The days were long and exhausting, but a newfound determination fueled me. I pushed myself beyond my limits, enduring the pain and fatigue with gritted teeth. Slowly but surely, progress emerged. My right arm began to respond, my leg regained some strength, and my speech became more fluid.

I also began to confront the emotional toll of my stroke. The fear, frustration, and overwhelming sense of loss all bubbled to the surface. With the help of a therapist, I learned to process these emotions and to accept the new reality I faced.

After months of relentless effort, the therapists deemed me ready to return home. It was a bittersweet moment, filled with both joy and trepidation. I was excited to be reunited with my family and friends, but I was also apprehensive about the challenges that lay ahead.

On January 13, 2021, I walked out of the rehabilitation center a changed man. I was weaker and slower, and my speech still faltered at times, but I was alive. I had faced death and emerged on the other side, forever altered but not defeated.

The journey back to normalcy was far from over. I continued with outpatient therapy, adapting to my new limitations and learning to navigate a world that suddenly seemed less accessible. But I was no longer alone. My family and friends rallied around me, offering unwavering support and encouragement.

The experience had irrevocably changed me. I was more grateful for the small things, appreciative of my loved ones, and determined to live life to the fullest. I had discovered a newfound strength within myself, a resilience I never knew I possessed.

Turning the Tide

And as I continued to heal, I knew that my story could inspire others facing similar challenges. I resolved to share my experience to offer hope and encouragement to those who had lost their way.

My journey through illness and recovery had been difficult, but it had also been transformative. It taught me the true meaning of strength, the power of determination, and the unwavering love of family and friends. It has shown me that even in the darkest times, there is always light at the end of the tunnel.

As the months passed, I found new ways to channel my energy and newfound perspective. I began to journal my experiences, capturing not only the physical milestones but also the emotional and mental hurdles. Writing became a form of therapy, allowing me to process my thoughts and reflect on my progress.

One afternoon, an idea sparked as I was flipping through my journal. What if I could compile my journey into a book? A memoir that could serve as a beacon of hope for others navigating similar paths. The idea excited me, and I immediately set to work, sifting through my entries, organizing my thoughts, and outlining the chapters.

The process of writing the memoir was cathartic but intense in its nature. Each word I penned was a step towards healing, a way to make sense of the chaos that had upended my life. I poured my heart into those pages, sharing the highs and lows of my recovery and the lessons I had learned about resilience, faith, and the indomitable human spirit.

As the manuscript took shape, I contacted a few friends and family members, asking them to read drafts and provide feedback. Their invaluable encouragement and support reinforced my belief that this story must be told. With their input, I refined the narrative, ensuring it was honest and inspirational.

Finally, after months of diligent work, the memoir was complete. I titled it "The Power of Faith," a reflection of my transformative journey. With the help of a friend in the publishing industry, I submitted the manuscript to several publishers. The waiting game began, filled with a mixture of hope and anxiety.

Turning the Tide

While awaiting responses, I continued my advocacy work. I spoke at local events, sharing my story with anyone listening. Each engagement was an opportunity to connect with others, to offer support and encouragement, and to raise awareness about stroke prevention and recovery.

One evening, as I was preparing for a talk at a nearby community center, my phone buzzed with an email notification. It was from a publisher. My heart raced as I opened the email, scanning the words with bated breath. They loved the manuscript and wanted to publish it.

The news was surreal. The journey that had begun in the sterile confines of the ICU was now culminating in a published work. I felt a deep sense of fulfillment, knowing that my story would reach a wider audience, touching lives and offering hope for many other souls.

# Chapter 6

## Homeward Bound

_"Let us hold fast the profession of our faith
without wavering."_

— Hebrews 10:23

Leaving the hospital felt like being handed a new lease on life. The gravity of my situation weighed heavily on me, but so did a profound sense of gratitude. It was as though God had blessed me with a second chance, and I was determined to make the most of it. More than just surviving, I wanted to live a life that could inspire others, showing them perseverance, faith, and determination could overcome even the darkest times.

## Homeward Bound

The days following my discharge from the rehabilitation center were a whirlwind of emotions. I was overjoyed to be home, embraced by the warmth and love of my family and friends, but there was also a sense of uncertainty. The journey ahead was still daunting, and I knew that the path to full recovery would be long and challenging.

Determined to regain my strength, I threw myself into physical therapy with unwavering commitment. Progress was slow, and there were days when the frustration felt overwhelming, but every small victory—every step taken without assistance—was a reminder that I was moving forward. Though seemingly insignificant, these moments filled me with a deep sense of accomplishment and renewed my resolve to keep pushing.

## Homeward Bound

Before leaving Boone Hospital, I was introduced to a rehabilitation facility in Kansas City called Ability KC. Despite the two-hour drive, I made the trip thrice a week, leaving home at 6 a.m. to arrive by 8 a.m. My dedication to recovery was unshakable. The first day at the facility involved a series of physical and mental assessments to tailor a rehabilitation program specifically for me. Given my desire to return to teaching math, the cognitive exercises focused on refining my math skills, again preparing me for the classroom.

To address the paralysis on my left side, the therapists employed small electrical currents designed to help my brain reconnect with the affected limbs. The breakthrough came when I was finally deemed ready to start walking again.

# Homeward Bound

The facility had an exoskeleton that guided my movements, ensuring I could only take a step if my body followed the correct sequence. This machine was instrumental in re-teaching me how to walk, making sure that every step was deliberate and precise.

As my strength and mobility improved, my thoughts shifted toward the future. I knew that returning to the classroom wouldn't happen immediately, but I was eager to find other ways to continue making a positive impact on the lives of others. One day, while browsing online, I discovered a Master's program in Curriculum & Instruction: Teaching Technology at Northwest Missouri State University. The program's focus on integrating technology into the classroom resonated with me deeply, aligning perfectly with my goal of becoming a more innovative educator. I had always been passionate about using technology to enhance learning, and this program seemed like the ideal path forward.

When I received the acceptance letter on January 31, 2023, it felt like a new beginning. This was not just another step in my career but a commitment to a future where I could share my passion for technology and education with others. The program was demanding, requiring countless study hours, research, and collaboration with fellow students. I delved into the latest educational technologies, explored innovative teaching strategies, and gained a deeper understanding of how technology could transform the educational landscape.

## Homeward Bound

During my time at Northwest, I experienced a mix of excitement and apprehension. It had been several years since I last walked the halls of the university, and I wasn't sure if I would recognize anyone. However, to my delight, I found that several of my former classmates from my undergraduate days were also pursuing their Master's degrees. Reconnecting with them brought a sense of comfort and nostalgia as we reminisced about our shared experiences.

An unexpected but wonderful surprise was discovering that my sister-in-law was also enrolled in a Master's program at Northwest, though in a different field. We ended up taking some of the same courses, albeit at various times, and our academic journeys became intertwined. We frequently compared notes, shared study tips, and supported each other through the more challenging moments of our studies. Her encouragement was invaluable, especially when the workload felt overwhelming.

The stroke left me with partial left-side paralysis, making it challenging to type papers and participate in online discussions. Initially, this was a significant obstacle, and I often felt frustrated and defeated. However, giving up was never an option. After some research, I discovered that voice-to-text software lets me directly dictate my thoughts and ideas to the computer. This tool was a game-changer, enabling me to complete assignments more efficiently and effectively without being hindered by physical limitations.

## Homeward Bound

As I progressed through the Master's program, I reflected on my decision to pursue further education at Northwest. Several factors influenced my choice. My undergraduate experience at Northwest was exceptional—the professors were knowledgeable and supportive, and the curriculum was challenging and engaging. I knew that returning to this institution would provide me with a high-quality education that would prepare me for a successful career in education.

Moreover, I learned that because I had graduated with a Bachelor's degree from Northwest, I wouldn't need to take the entrance exam for the Master's program, saving me both time and effort. I also felt confident about my academic record—having graduated with Cum

Laude Honors and a 3.5 GPA, I was sure that my grades would meet the program's requirements.

After graduating in December 2020, I quickly began my teaching career at South Harrison School District, eager to apply my knowledge and skills in the classroom. However, the stroke I suffered in November 2021 forced me to step back from teaching and focus on my recovery. During this time, I realized that my passion for making a difference in others' lives hadn't diminished—I just needed to find a new way to channel it.

As I thought about the future, I knew that my ultimate goal was to return to the classroom, where my heart indeed lay. Teaching had always been my passion, and I was especially drawn to teaching 5th-grade math, where my teaching career had first begun. I loved the challenge of helping students build a strong foundation in mathematics, and I found immense satisfaction in watching them gain confidence in their abilities.

However, I was also open to new opportunities, including teaching business classes, as I was certified as a business teacher in Missouri. I believed my business knowledge and experience would be valuable in the classroom, and I was eager to share this passion with my students.

In addition to my teaching aspirations, I also dreamed of reviving my lawn-mowing business. Before my stroke, I had cherished the freedom and autonomy of being self-employed. The simple pleasure of the fresh scent of cut grass and the sense of accomplishment at the end of a hard day's work was genuinely invigorating. Mowing lawns provided me with extra income and allowed me to contribute to the upkeep of our property.

I was confident that I could successfully re-establish my mowing business with some adjustments and accommodations. It might require modifying my schedule or working slower, but I was determined to find a way to make it feasible.

I felt a deep sense of optimism as I looked toward the future. Despite my challenges, I believed I could achieve my goals and lead a fulfilling, purposeful life. My journey had taught me the value of perseverance and faith, and I was determined to make every day count.

I have always been reserved throughout my life, focusing more on my studies than extracurricular activities. I didn't participate much in intramural sports, but I excelled academically, graduating as valedictorian from Newtown-Harris High School with a GPA of 4.01. My academic success continued at North Central Missouri College, where I graduated with the Highest Honors and maintained a GPA just shy of 4.0. I was honored to be inducted into the academic chapter of Pi Omega Pi.

In addition to my academic achievements, I stayed connected to my faith by actively participating in a church organization called the Navigators. After a couple of years, I assumed the student leader role, allowing me to share my faith with fellow students on campus. I also became involved in The Association of Non-traditional Students. Before graduating, I had the privilege of serving as the vice president of both Pi Omega Pi and The Association of Non-traditional Students.

Looking back, I realized that every experience, every challenge, and every success had prepared me for this moment. My journey was far from over, but I was ready to face whatever came next, armed with the lessons I had learned and the unwavering belief that I could overcome any obstacle in my path.

Leaving the hospital wasn't just a physical transition; it began a profound emotional journey. Returning home, where everything felt familiar and strange, triggered a wave of emotions I hadn't fully anticipated. The comfort of my surroundings were contrasted with the overwhelming reality of my new physical limitations. Simple tasks, once quickly done, now require immense effort and patience. The stairs I had climbed countless times now loomed like a mountain, and the once-ordinary act of getting dressed had become a frustrating ordeal.

The mental struggle was equally challenging. There were days when the uncertainty of my future weighed heavily on my spirit. Would I ever be able to walk unaided again? Could I return to the classroom where I had found so much joy and purpose? These questions circled in my mind, sometimes eroding the resolve that I clung to so desperately. But in those dark moments, I found solace in my faith and the unwavering support of my family and friends. Their encouragement became the lifeline I needed, reminding me that I wasn't alone in this battle.

### Homeward Bound

The days and weeks after I began my Master's program at Northwest Missouri State University were both exhilarating and exhausting. Each new assignment brought a sense of purpose, a reminder that I was on a path toward something meaningful. Yet, the challenges were undeniable. My body was still healing, and there were days when my energy waned when the physical toll of my recovery made the academic workload feel like an insurmountable mountain.

But I had never been one to shy away from a challenge. In those moments of fatigue, I leaned on the support system I had carefully built around me—my family, friends, and classmates. Their encouragement was a constant source of strength. I began to see my journey not just as a personal battle but as a shared endeavor that involved everyone who had been by my side through the darkest days.

One of the most profound sources of support came from an unexpected place—my students. Even though I wasn't back in the classroom, I stayed in touch with many of them through occasional visits to sporting events. Their messages were full of well-wishes and updates on their lives, but more than that, they were full of hope. They saw me as an example, and that realization fueled my determination to succeed. I wasn't just doing this for myself; I was doing it for them to show them that setbacks are just that— not the end of the road.

I found a renewed sense of energy as winter gave way to spring. The rehabilitation sessions, which had once been grueling, began to feel more like steps in the right direction. The exoskeleton at Ability KC, once a machine that dictated my movements, became a tool of liberation. With each session, my gait became more natural, and my steps more confident. The day I walked a few steps without the aid of the exoskeleton was one I'll never forget. It was a victory that felt as monumental as any academic achievement.

With my physical recovery progressing, I also began to think more seriously about my future in education. The Master's program opened up new possibilities, expanding my vision of what I could do in the classroom. I started to dream about creating a curriculum that integrated technology in ways that hadn't been explored before. I envisioned a classroom where students used interactive tools to learn math concepts, where lessons were not confined to textbooks but brought to life through technology.

My experiences with voice-to-text software sparked another idea. I realized that technology could be a game-changer for students with disabilities, just as it had been for me. This insight fueled my passion for inclusive education, and I started researching ways to make my future classroom accessible to all students, regardless of their physical or cognitive abilities. I wanted to ensure that every student had the tools they needed to succeed, just as I had been given the tools to overcome my own challenges.

As I continued my studies, my thoughts often wandered to the day when I would return to teaching. I imagined standing in front of a classroom once again, feeling the familiar rush of excitement as I introduced a new concept to my students. But this time, there would be a difference. I would return with a deeper understanding of resilience, a story of survival and determination that I could share with my students. I hoped that my journey would inspire them, not just in their academic pursuits but in life itself.

The end of the academic year brought with it a sense of accomplishment. I had completed the first year of my Master's program, a milestone that felt particularly sweet given everything I had been through. But there was still more to come, more to learn, more to achieve. And I was ready for it. The future no longer seemed uncertain; it was a landscape of possibilities, and I was eager to explore it.

Homeward Bound

During the summer break, I took some time to reflect on how far I had come. The memory of the stroke, though still vivid, had become less about the trauma and more about the lessons it had taught me. I learned the value of patience, the importance of perseverance, and the power of faith. These lessons I knew would stay with me for the rest of my life, guiding me in my personal and professional journey.

In the quiet moments of that summer, I also revisited my dream of reviving my lawn-mowing business. The physical work of mowing lawns, which had once seemed impossible, now felt within reach. I began to plan, thinking about how I could manage the business while continuing my studies and my recovery. It was a daunting prospect, but the idea of returning to something I loved filled me with anticipation. I knew it would require careful balancing, but I was confident that I could make it work with determination and the suitable adjustments.

As the new school year approached, I felt a mix of excitement and nervousness. I knew that the road ahead would still have its challenges, but I was no longer the same person who had been discharged from the hospital months earlier. I was stronger, more determined, and ready to face whatever came next. I had a renewed sense of purpose and a deep belief in my ability to overcome any obstacles in my path.

The fall semester began with a sense of anticipation. The coursework was challenging, but I found myself thriving in the environment of learning and discovery. My professors were not just educators; they were mentors who supported my goals and encouraged my ambitions. They saw in me the potential to make a real impact in the field of education, and their belief in me only strengthened my resolve.

One day, while working on a project for one of my classes, I received an email that would change the course of my journey. It was an offer to collaborate on a research paper about the use of technology in special education. The opportunity was both exciting and intimidating, but I knew I couldn't pass it up. This was a chance to contribute to the field meaningfully to use my experiences to help others.

The research project consumed much of my time that semester but was a labor of love. I spent hours in the library, poring over studies and articles and typing up drafts and revisions late at night. The work was challenging, but it was also deeply fulfilling. For the first time since the stroke, I felt like I was not just recovering but genuinely thriving. I was contributing to something larger than myself, and it felt incredible.

As the semester drew to a close, I submitted the final version of our paper. It was accepted for publication, and I felt the sense of pride and accomplishment was overwhelming. This was more than just a paper; it was a testament to my journey, the strength I had found within myself, and the support of everyone who had helped me along the way.

Looking ahead, I knew that my journey was far from over. There were still many challenges to face, both in my recovery and in my career. But I was no longer daunted by them. Instead, I saw them as opportunities to grow, learn, and make a difference. I was ready to take on whatever came next, confident in navigating the twists and turns of the road ahead.

As I prepared for the next chapter of my life, I felt a deep sense of gratitude. Gratitude for the second chance I was given, the people who supported me, and the journey that brought me to this point. I knew that I had been blessed, and I was determined to use that blessing to inspire others, to show them that no matter how difficult the road may be, it is always possible to find your way home.

# Chapter 7

## College Life

Choosing Northwest Missouri State University in Maryville, MO, was a pivotal decision in my life. It wasn't just about furthering my academic career but seizing the chance to immerse myself in a thriving campus culture while nurturing my faith. Northwest accepted most of the credit hours I had earned at North Central Missouri College, making it the ideal next step on my educational journey. However, I quickly realized that the university experience was far more than just attending classes—it was about the community, the friendships, and the opportunities for personal growth that awaited beyond the classroom walls.

## College Life

I knew I wanted to stay strong in my Christian faith from the beginning. On campus, I found solace and a sense of belonging through a Christian group called the Navigators. The Navigators were a welcoming community committed to evangelizing to students across Northwest's campus. Their warmth and dedication to faith resonated with me, and I became increasingly involved with their activities as the year progressed. Toward the end of the year, they began discussing a summer mission trip to Jacksonville, Florida, which they affectionately called "Jax." Intrigued by their stories, I couldn't help but be drawn in. The idea of spending three months in Jacksonville, evangelizing on the beaches of the Atlantic Ocean, was too exciting to pass up.

## College Life

As the details of the trip unfolded, my anticipation grew. Little did I know that this adventure would become one of the most transformative experiences of my life. The Navigators took about 100 students from Northwest—one of the largest campus groups to participate in Jax that summer. The logistics of transporting such a large group across several states were daunting, but it also added to the excitement. We divided it into three caravans, each consisting of five or six vehicles, and set off on the long journey south. Over the course of three days, we made pit stops at large churches in Clarksville, Tennessee, and somewhere in Georgia (the exact location escapes me). Finally, we arrived at the scenic University of Northern

Florida (UNF), which would be our home for the summer.

In Jacksonville, our mission was to spread our faith and broaden our reach by integrating into the local community through various jobs. I ended up securing a job with a moving company, which provided a unique perspective on the lives of the people in the area. We were tasked with loading and unloading furniture from storage units. While the work could be grueling—especially in the humid Florida heat—the refreshing ocean breeze often made it bearable. Through this job, I gained a newfound appreciation for the physical demands of labor and the importance of teamwork.

The friendships I formed that summer were unlike any I had experienced before. Initially, I gravitated toward the familiar faces of my Northwest friends, but as the weeks passed, I found myself growing closer to those in my study group. These were people I might never have met otherwise, and our shared experiences in Jacksonville forged bonds that would last a lifetime. We spent countless hours together, whether on the beach evangelizing, participating in Bible studies, or simply enjoying the beauty of our surroundings. By the end of the summer, they felt like family.

Back at Northwest, the university was renowned for its athletic prowess, and I eagerly embraced the campus sports culture. I vividly recall attending numerous football and basketball games, where the stands were always packed with enthusiastic fans. The energy of the student section was infectious, making every game an unforgettable experience. Whether it was a nail-biting finish or a landslide victory, the sense of camaraderie among the students was palpable. Being part of that collective energy was thrilling and reminded me that college was about more than just academics—it was about being part of something bigger.

To support myself financially, I juggled several part-time jobs during my time at Northwest. One of my main gigs was working at a manufacturing plant in Maryville. The work was challenging, but it taught me valuable lessons about the industrial sector and the importance of perseverance. When I wasn't at the plant, I dabbled in the gig economy by becoming an Uber driver and a delivery driver for a food delivery service. With its small population of around 12,000, Maryville didn't always provide enough business, so I frequently ventured to St. Joseph, Missouri—a larger city with a population of approximately 76,000—to boost my earnings. The hustle and bustle of St. Joseph contrasted sharply with the quiet of Maryville, but it allowed me to interact with a diverse range of people and gain insights into different walks of life.

These varied experiences—whether it was working in the moving industry, driving through the streets of Missouri, or sharing my faith on the beaches of Jacksonville—enriched my understanding of the world. They taught me the value of adaptability, hard work, and human connection. Every interaction and every challenge I faced added another layer to my personal growth.

As I approached the end of my college years, I felt a deep sense of accomplishment. The stroke I had suffered had undoubtedly been a life-altering event, but it had also opened my eyes to the fragility of life and the power of resilience. My experiences at Northwest and beyond had prepared me for whatever challenges lay ahead. I was grateful for the support of my loving family, loyal friends, and a community that believed in me every step of the way.

Returning to the classroom as a teacher now seemed like a natural progression of my journey. I envisioned a future where I could use my knowledge and experiences to empower and inspire the next generation of students. I wanted to be more than just an educator—I wanted to be a mentor who could guide others through their challenges and help them realize their potential.

Beyond the classroom, I was eager to revive my lawn-mowing business. It might seem like a small endeavor, but I believe that even the smallest acts of service could make a meaningful difference in the lives of others. I saw it as an opportunity to contribute to my community's well-being and lead by example.

Looking ahead, I was filled with a sense of hope and anticipation. The future was uncertain, but I knew I was equipped to face whatever came my way. With unwavering faith in God's guidance and a deep sense of purpose, I was ready to embrace the next chapter of my life. My story was far from over, and I was determined to continue writing it with courage, perseverance, and the belief that I would never give up, no matter the obstacles.

As I navigated the complexities of college life, I often grappled with questions of identity and purpose. Northwest offered more than academic challenges; it was a place where I was forced to confront who I indeed was and what I wanted out of life. The pressure to excel academically, maintain my faith, and fit into the social fabric of college life sometimes felt overwhelming. There were nights when I would lie awake, wondering if I was on the right path. What did success really mean? Was it about grades, social status, or something deeper? My faith became a cornerstone during these times, offering clarity and comfort. I prayed for guidance, seeking answers to the more significant questions that weighed on my mind. Slowly, through moments of introspection and quiet reflection, I began to realize that my purpose was not tied to external achievements but to the impact I could have on others.

During one particularly challenging semester, I met a professor who would become a pivotal figure in my life. Dr. Thompson, who taught philosophy, was known for his unconventional approach to teaching. He encouraged us to question everything to dig deeper into our beliefs and assumptions. After class one day, I approached him, seeking advice on balancing my faith with the academic world, which often seemed at odds with it. We ended up talking for hours. Dr. Thompson shared his own journey of reconciling faith with intellectual curiosity. He spoke about the importance of embracing doubt to strengthen belief and how true growth often comes from confronting uncomfortable truths. His words resonated with me, and from that day on, our conversations became a regular part of my college experience. Dr. Thompson's mentorship helped me see that my faith and education weren't in conflict; they were complementary paths guiding me toward a fuller understanding of the world and my place in it.

One of the most defining moments of my college years occurred during the Jacksonville trip. It was a humid afternoon, and our group had been evangelizing on the beach for hours. I started a conversation with a man who seemed lost in thought, sitting alone by the shore. His name was Tony, and as we talked, I learned that he was struggling with deep personal pain—grieving the loss of his wife and feeling disconnected from his faith. Listening to Tony's story touched me in a way I hadn't expected. He wasn't just another person we were trying to reach; he was someone whose pain mirrored the uncertainties I had felt in my own life. We talked for a long time, and by the end of our conversation, there was a shared sense of peace. It wasn't just about the words we exchanged but the connection we forged through understanding. That encounter stayed with me long after the summer ended. It reminded me that our faith journeys are profoundly personal and that sometimes, simply being present for someone else can be the most potent form of ministry.

## College Life

As I looked back on my time at Northwest, what stood out most wasn't the classes or the football games, though both were memorable. It was the community I had found—through the Navigators, through my study groups, and through the jobs that pushed me out of my comfort zone. There was a particular moment during my final year that epitomized the importance of that community. I had been going through a tough time, feeling the weight of impending graduation and the uncertainty of the future. One evening, a few friends from my study group surprised me with a small gathering. They had noticed I wasn't quite myself lately and wanted to lift my spirits. We spent hours talking, laughing, and simply being there for one another. That night reminded me that no matter how independent I tried to be, it was okay to lean on others. In fact, it was necessary. The relationships I built at Northwest were the proper foundation of my college experience, and they were what gave me the strength to face the future with confidence.

# Chapter 8

## Resilience

The year 2022 was full of ups and downs. As I reflect on the journey that began with my hospitalization at Boone, I am struck by the resilience of the human spirit and the profound impact that faith can have in guiding us through the darkest times. The stroke I suffered in November 2021 was more than just a medical emergency—it was a stark reminder of life's fragility, the preciousness of every moment, and the need to hold on to hope, even when faced with the unimaginable. But it was also a testament to the power of perseverance, the strength that comes from within, and the unwavering support of loved ones, healthcare professionals, and, above all, the grace of God that carried me through.

After my discharge from Boone Hospital, I entered a period of profound uncertainty. The physical and emotional toll of the stroke had left me in a state of limbo—grateful for the progress I had made, yet acutely aware that the road ahead was still long and uncharted. I wasn't yet cleared to return to my beloved teaching profession, and the thought of being away from the classroom, where I had always found purpose and fulfillment, weighed heavily on my heart. The classroom had been my sanctuary, the place where I felt most alive, most connected to my purpose. To be separated from that world was to feel adrift, unsure of how to navigate the days ahead. Yet, I knew that healing could not be rushed. To return too soon would be to risk my long-term well-being, so I made the difficult decision to place my trust in the process, allowing time and patience to do their work.

June 10, 2022—a date that started with hope and excitement- was another turning point in my challenging journey. I was on my way to a music festival called Resound Fest in Bethany, MO. The air was warm, filled with the promise of joy and a brief escape from my troubles. I could feel myself getting stronger, my spirit lifting as I anticipated the music, the crowd, the energy. We quickly stopped at a gas station in Princeton, MO, for some snacks. I remember reaching for a bag of chips, and just as I was about to check out, a strange sensation washed over me. My heartbeat pounded in my ears, my vision blurred, and I felt myself leaning uncontrollably to the right.

I heard my mom's voice, laced with panic, calling for someone to dial 911. In what felt like seconds, I was being loaded into an ambulance, my mind foggy and disoriented. The attending technician was severe but calm. "You've had a major seizure," he said, and his words hung heavy in the air as the ambulance raced towards Wright Memorial Hospital in Trenton, MO.

As the days passed, a new pain emerged— sharp, nagging discomfort in my right shoulder. An MRI revealed that I had re-aggravated and extended a tear in my right labrum. This was my good shoulder, my one reliable side, unaffected by the stroke. Surgery was an option, but I knew it would leave me completely immobilized. It wasn't just fear—it was survival. I couldn't afford to lose the use of my good side, even temporarily. I decided to go for physical therapy instead, hoping it would be enough.

Each session was a mix of hope and agony. The therapist worked meticulously, helping me strengthen my arm and increase its mobility. Pain flared with every movement, but I persisted. Gradually, strength returned to my shoulder, and the pain that had once been my constant companion began to fade. By the end, I could move without flinching, my shoulder no longer screaming with every lift and turn. It was a small victory, but a victory nonetheless.

Yet, 2022 had more in store for me. On October 1, 2022, I woke up drenched in sweat, my stomach clenched in a vise of unbearable pain. It was as if a thousand knives were twisting inside me. Panic set in, and we rushed to the emergency room. The nurses, seeing my condition, swiftly moved me through for a CT scan. The verdict: gallstones. The sharp agony I felt was due to a stone shifting, triggering the excruciating pain that jolted me awake.

The doctor's advice was clear: "Gallstones have a way of coming back," he said. "It's best to remove the gallbladder to avoid future complications." I agreed to the surgery scheduled for October 4, 2022. The operation went smoothly, but it was late in the day. The decision was made to keep me overnight for observation, just in case. That night, I lay in the sterile hospital bed, feeling a strange sense of calm. For once, nothing went wrong; the night was uneventful, and I was discharged the following morning.

Each of these moments was a test of endurance, a test of spirit, a test of faith. And though I stumbled and faltered, I did not fall. Each challenge only strengthened my resolve and solidified my determination to reclaim my life.

Thus began my journey of rehabilitation—a journey that was not just physical but also profoundly psychological and emotional. Each day presented new challenges, but I grew stronger in both body and spirit with each small victory. My physical therapy sessions became battlegrounds where I fought tirelessly to regain strength and mobility. Every step, every stretch, every repetition was a testament to my determination to reclaim the life I had known.

## Resilience

Occupational therapy became a lesson in patience, teaching me to persevere as I relearned simple tasks I had once taken for granted. And speech therapy became my lifeline, helping me to reclaim my voice, both literally and figuratively, as I worked to regain the ability to communicate clearly and confidently.

But the rehabilitation process was not solely about restoring my physical capabilities—it was also a deep introspection and self-discovery journey. In the long hours of therapy and reflection, I often found myself contemplating the deeper meaning behind my ordeal. Why had this happened to me? What lessons could I learn from this experience? These questions lingered in my mind, guiding me toward a deeper understanding of resilience and embracing adversity as an opportunity for growth. I realized that while I could not control the circumstances of my life, I could choose how I responded to them. I could choose to see my challenges not as insurmountable obstacles but as stepping stones on the path to becoming a stronger, more compassionate version of myself.

One of the most profound realizations that emerged during this time was the significance of gratitude. Despite my many hardships, I was surrounded by abundant blessings—loving family and friends who lifted me when I was at my lowest, dedicated healthcare professionals who guided me with care and expertise, and a community that enveloped me with kindness and support. Each day became an opportunity to practice gratitude, to find joy in the small moments that might otherwise have gone unnoticed—a gentle breeze on a sunny day, the laughter of loved ones, the warmth of a comforting embrace. Gratitude became my anchor, grounding me in the present and helping me see the beauty that still existed in my life, even amid uncertainty.

And then there was faith—the unshakable belief that I was not alone even in my darkest moments. My faith became a beacon of hope, illuminating the path ahead when all else seemed uncertain. I leaned heavily on my faith throughout this journey, drawing strength from the knowledge that I was being held in the loving embrace of a higher power. Even in my weakest moments, I felt the presence of God guiding me forward with grace and compassion, reminding me that, with Him, all things are possible. This unwavering faith sustained me through the toughest times, giving me the courage to keep moving forward, even when the road seemed impossibly long.

As I worked toward reclaiming my health, my thoughts began to turn toward the future. What lay ahead for me once I was deemed fit to return to work? How could I take this experience and use it to become not only a better teacher but also a beacon of resilience and hope for my students? These questions weighed heavily on my mind, and as I pondered them, a new idea began to take root—the idea of pursuing further education. It was a seed that had been planted long ago, but it was only now, in the wake of my recovery, that it began to flourish. The thought of returning to school of expanding my knowledge and skill set filled me with a renewed sense of purpose. It seemed like the perfect way to honor the journey I had been on, to take the lessons I had learned and use them to make a meaningful impact on the lives of others.

With a heart of hope and determination, I applied to the Master's program in **Curriculum & Instruction: Teaching Technology.** This program represented a new beginning for me, a chance to delve into innovative teaching methods and explore how technology could be harnessed to enhance student learning. The prospect of immersing myself in these new ideas and tools filled me with excitement and anticipation. I saw it as an opportunity not just to adapt to the changes in education but to embrace them fully, knowing that the future of teaching would be shaped by our ability to innovate and evolve.

## Resilience

As I began my studies, I found solace in pursuing knowledge. Each lesson, each assignment, and each new concept was a step forward on my journey of self-discovery and growth. The challenges I encountered along the way only served to strengthen my resolve. I was no longer the same person I had been before the stroke—this journey had changed me in ways I could never have imagined. But as I moved through the program, I realized that these changes were not something to be feared but embraced. I was becoming a more resilient, adaptable, and compassionate educator, and I knew that this new version of myself would be better equipped to serve my students and help them navigate their challenges with grace and determination.

## Resilience

Now, as I approach the culmination of my Master's degree journey in December of 2024, I can't help but feel an overwhelming sense of pride and accomplishment. It has been a long and arduous road, marked by setbacks and challenges but also by moments of triumph and joy. And through it all, one constant has remained—the guiding hand of God, whose grace has sustained me through every trial and every victory. This journey has taught me that resilience is not just about bouncing back from adversity; it is about embracing the journey itself, finding strength in the struggle, and trusting that, no matter what lies ahead, we have the power to endure and thrive.

As I continued this journey, I became acutely aware of the importance of purpose in recovery.

## Resilience

There were days when progress felt agonizingly slow, and I questioned whether I would ever return to the life I once knew. During these moments, I realized how critical it was to have something to strive toward. Having goals gave me a reason to push through the tough days, to get up and attend therapy even when my body felt weak and tired. But beyond the immediate goal of physical recovery, I found that reconnecting with my purpose as an educator and a lifelong learner reignited my spirit. The decision to pursue further education to expand my horizons became a light at the end of the tunnel—a beacon guiding me toward a future filled with possibilities.

The stroke forced me to reconsider my relationship with time. Life had once been rushed, filled with deadlines, commitments, and responsibilities that often left little room for rest or reflection. But now, time seemed to stretch out in front of me, slow and deliberate. I learned to be patient with myself and honor the healing process rather than rush through it. This newfound relationship with time extended beyond my recovery—it reshaped how I approached every aspect of my life. I began prioritizing moments of stillness and introspection, finding value in slowing down and truly being present in the moment. This shift in perspective aided my healing and brought a more profound sense of peace and contentment to my everyday life.

Through this journey, I also discovered the profound impact of creativity on healing. As someone who had always found joy in teaching and learning, I turned to creative outlets as a form of therapy. Writing became more than just a way to document my journey—it became a way to express the emotions that were too complex for words alone. I also explored new hobbies, such as painting and photography, which allowed me to tap into a part of myself that was both healing and liberating. These creative endeavors reminded me that healing isn't just about physical recovery—it's about nourishing the soul, finding beauty in the world around you, and reconnecting with the passions that bring you joy.

One of the unexpected gifts of this experience was the opportunity to forge new connections with others who had gone through similar challenges. I became part of a community of stroke survivors, people who understood the unique struggles and triumphs of recovery in a way that no one else could. I found a sense of camaraderie and solidarity that was incredibly healing through support groups, online forums, and personal conversations. These connections allowed me to see that I was not alone in my journey and that there was strength in sharing our stories and lifting each other. The bonds I formed within this community became integral to my recovery, reminding me that resilience is often found in the collective power of shared experiences.

As I moved further along this path, I began envisioning new possibilities for my future. While my passion for teaching remained steadfast, I saw how my resilience journey could open doors to new opportunities. I became interested in advocacy work, particularly raising awareness about stroke prevention and recovery. Using my voice and my story to help others avoid or overcome similar challenges was empowering and humbling. I started to explore ways to combine my love for education with my newfound commitment to advocacy, envisioning a future where I could inspire change both in and out of the classroom.

Finally, this resilience journey led me to a deeper understanding of mind, body, and spirit interconnectedness. I realized that true healing requires a holistic approach that addresses not just the physical aspects of recovery but also the emotional, mental, and spiritual dimensions of well-being. This understanding inspired me to incorporate mindfulness, meditation, and spiritual reflection into my daily routine. By nurturing all aspects of myself, I cultivated a sense of balance and harmony crucial to my recovery. This holistic approach to healing is something I now carry with me, not just as a tool for recovery but as a way of living—a way of being fully present in my own life, attuned to the needs of my body, mind, and spirit.

As I look toward the future, I am filled with a sense of anticipation for the new chapters that lie ahead. I know that life will continue to present challenges, but I also know that I am equipped to handle them with grace and resilience. The lessons I have learned on this journey have become an integral part of who I am, shaping my outlook on life and how I engage with the world around me. I am ready to embrace whatever comes next, confident in my ability to navigate it with strength, faith, and an unyielding commitment to growth.

# Chapter 9

## Uncertainty

Looking ahead, my goal remains unwavering: to return to the classroom not merely as a teacher but as a beacon of hope, a living testament to resilience, and an inspiration to every student who walks through my doors. The road I've traveled has been riddled with trials. Still, each obstacle has reinforced the profound power of faith, the necessity of perseverance, and the indomitable nature of the human spirit. As I prepare to take my next steps forward, I do so with a heart brimming with gratitude and a renewed sense of purpose. I am fully aware that all things are possible with God by my side. Glory to God, indeed, for His steadfast love and unwavering grace have carried me through the darkest storms and into the light of a new day. As I embark on this next chapter of my life, I do so with faith as my compass and hope as my guiding star. In His strength, I find my own; in His love, I find the courage to face challenges.

Yet, the path to this clarity has been anything but smooth. It all began on that fateful day, June 10, 2022. My heart was light, and my spirit was high as I set out for Resound Fest, a music festival in the serene town of Bethany, Missouri. Music had always been a source of joy and healing for me, and I looked forward to the uplifting atmosphere that awaited. Little did I know, fate had other plans.

As we made our way to the festival, we decided to make a quick stop at a gas station in the quaint town of Princeton, Missouri. It was supposed to be a simple, uneventful pause in our journey. But as I stood in line with snacks in hand, I suddenly felt dread. My heartbeat pounded in my ears, growing louder with each passing second. My vision blurred, and I felt myself leaning uncontrollably to my right. Panic set in as I realized I could not stop myself from falling. The world around me dimmed, and I last remember hearing my mother's frantic voice calling out for help.

What happened next remains a blur. I was loaded into an ambulance, my mother's terrified face the last thing I saw before the doors closed. The attending technician, his voice steady yet grave, informed me that I had suffered a major seizure. The words hung in the air like a death sentence. A major seizure? I had always been the strong one, the resilient one. How could this be happening to me?

The next few days were a whirlwind of confusion, pain, and fear. As if the seizure hadn't been enough, a few days later, I began to experience intense pain in my right shoulder. An MRI revealed the harsh reality: I had re-aggravated and extended the tear in my right labrum. This was a devastating blow, as this was my good shoulder, the one part of me that had remained unaffected by the stroke. The idea of undergoing surgery was unbearable. I couldn't face the thought of being completely immobilized, so I decided against it. I was determined to fight through the pain, to prove that I was stronger than this affliction.

## Uncertainty

I sought the help of a local physical therapist, a woman whose hands seemed to work miracles. She focused on strengthening my arm, increasing its mobility, and alleviating the pain that had become a constant companion. The sessions were excruciating, each movement a battle against my own body. But slowly, painfully, I regained mobility and strength in my right shoulder. The pain that had once been unbearable started to fade. For the first time in weeks, I could go through the day without wincing with every movement. I even managed to walk without a cane, though the effects of the seizure had set my recovery back significantly. Still, I pressed on, determined to reclaim my life, one step at a time.

## Uncertainty

But the challenges were far from over. On October 1, 2022, another crisis struck. I awoke in the middle of the night, drenched in sweat and doubled over in excruciating pain. My stomach felt as if it were being torn apart from the inside. Panic gripped me as I realized something was terribly wrong. We rushed to the emergency room, my mind racing with fear and uncertainty. What could possibly be happening to me now?

At the hospital, the nurses quickly whisked me away for a CT scan. The diagnosis was swift and merciless: gallstones. These tiny, jagged stones had moved, causing the unimaginable pain that had jolted me from sleep. The doctors informed me that if I had gallstones once, I was likely to have them again. The only way to prevent future agony was to have my gallbladder removed. The decision was made quickly, and the surgery was scheduled for October 4.

The surgery was a blur of bright lights, cold metal, and distant voices. It went well, or as the doctors said, but because it was performed so late, they decided to keep me overnight for observation. The night was long, filled with a strange mix of relief and anxiety. I was grateful that the surgery had gone smoothly, but the uncertainty of what lay ahead weighed heavily on my mind.

The following morning, I was released from the hospital, physically intact but emotionally drained. The events of the past few months had taken their toll. Once solid and capable, my body felt like a fragile, easily broken vessel. But as I walked out of the hospital, I realized something profound: I was still here. I had faced the storm and came out the other side. Weaker, perhaps, but alive.

And so, as I look to the future, I do so with a heavy and hopeful heart. I know that the road ahead will not be easy, but I also know that I am not walking it alone. With God as my guide, I will continue to push forward, reclaim my life, and fulfill my purpose. For in His strength, I find my own; in His love, I find the courage to face whatever challenges lie ahead. All glory to God, indeed, for carrying me through the storm and into the light of a new day.

# Chapter 10

## NYR - A Journey of Faith and Fellowship

"For where two or three gather in my name, there am I with them." – Matthew 18:20

You might imagine campfires, cabins, and familiar faces when you think of summer camps. But NYR, or Nationwide Youth Roundup, is no ordinary summer camp. It uniquely blends faith, fellowship, and the rugged outdoors. Held every summer in the mountains, about 20 miles from Castle Rock, Colorado, NYR, is a powerful reminder of what it means to step away from the hustle of daily life and into a sacred space where God is at the center of everything.

NYR – A Journey of Faith and Fellowship

NYR runs from the last week of July into the first week of August and attracts churches from all over the United States. Each church group makes the long drive, not just for a retreat but for an experience that will test their physical strength, deepen their faith, and forge lifelong friendships. What sets NYR apart is the raw, rustic environment—camp attendees build their own campsites and live in tents for the entire week. There are no pre-built cabins or easy comforts; it's a place where you work with your hands, sleep under the stars, and worship with fellow believers from across the country.

The camp schedule revolves around two main sessions, one in the morning and one in the afternoon. These sessions are filled with vibrant worship music led by live bands, followed by

NYR – A Journey of Faith and Fellowship passionate speakers who preach on a wide range of spiritual topics. Each sermon is a call to reflect on faith, personal growth, and how we live out our relationship with Christ. After the morning session, campers break off into classes tailored for different age groups, allowing everyone to engage deeply with the Word in a way that resonates with their life stage.

But NYR is not just about the formal sessions. Once the morning classes wrap up, the rest of the day is free for relaxation, sports, or simply connecting with others. It's during these moments that the heart of NYR truly shines. Campers are encouraged to mingle, share their stories, and learn from one another. People from vastly different walks of life, brought together by their

NYR – A Journey of Faith and Fellowship

shared faith, form connections that transcend geography and time.

I first attended NYR in the summer of 2000, an experience that left a lasting mark on my life. That year, my church decided to participate alone for the first time, which meant we were responsible for setting up our entire campsite from scratch. The process wasn't easy. We weren't allowed to cut down trees, so the early crew—including myself—had to gather fallen logs and use pickaxes to break up the dirt. It was hard work but incredibly rewarding. Something is humbling about preparing a place where others can come and find shelter, where fellowship and faith can flourish.

Every year, a group from our church heads out early to set up the campsite for the rest of us.

They don't just pitch tents—they create a home for the week. They assemble a cooking tent and a dining area and even hang tarps over the tents to protect them from the elements. It's a labor of love, and by the time the rest of the group arrives, the campsite feels like a little village, ready to welcome each person into the community.

What makes NYR truly special for me is the people. Every summer, you meet campers from all across the United States—people with different stories, backgrounds, and journeys of faith. Conversations come quickly because there's so much to share. Even more remarkable is that you can go a whole year without seeing someone, but the moment you reconnect at NYR, it's as if no time has passed. Friendships at NYR are unique

NYR – A Journey of Faith and Fellowship
because they are built on shared experiences and
a common bond in Christ.

I look forward to seeing familiar faces each
summer and making new connections. When they
announce the dates for the next NYR, I mark it on
my calendar and start a countdown on my phone.
That anticipation of something more significant on
the horizon keeps me returning year after year.

Another aspect of NYR that I treasure is the
opportunity to disconnect. In today's world, we are
constantly bombarded with distractions—our
phones, social media, and the never-ending
demands of daily life. But at NYR, there's hardly
any cell service. At first, it's a shock to the system,
but soon it becomes a blessing. Without the
constant buzz of notifications, I find myself more
attuned to the people around me and, more

importantly, to God. The absence of digital noise creates a space for reflection, prayer, and genuine spiritual growth. It's a rare opportunity to be fully present with the people around you and the Lord.

In many ways, NYR is more than just a church camp. It's a journey of faith, friendship, and discovery. It's a place where you come face to face with the raw beauty of creation, where hard work is a part of the spiritual experience, and where each year feels like a homecoming. The mountains become a sanctuary, the people your brothers and sisters in Christ, and the lessons learned are carried long after

Reflecting on my NYR experiences, I realize it's not just about the week in the mountains. It's about the way that week shapes the rest of your year. The teachings, friendships, and moments of worship all leave a lasting imprint on your heart. And as soon as one year's camp ends, the anticipation for the next one begins. Because I know, without a doubt, that when two or three—or in this case, hundreds—gather in His name, God is truly there among us.

www.ingramcontent.com/pod-product-compliance
Lightning Source LLC
Chambersburg PA
CBHW062108080426
42734CB00012B/2796